Farting Santa's Festive Coloring Frenzy"

Ho, ho, hold onto your giggles, because Farting Santa has arrived in town, and he's bringing the funniest, merriest, and most festive coloring book ever!

Step into the world of Farting Santa, where holiday cheer meets good-natured guffaws. Santa Claus might be known for delivering presents and ho-ho-ho-ing, but in this coloring book, he's also known for a unique talent — spreading joy with his jolly toots! Get ready for a burst of laughter and a whole lot of color.

In these pages, you'll find Santa Claus and his loyal reindeer, not only dashing through the snow but also sharing a chuckle or two along the way. This holiday season, they're celebrating with a symphony of silly sounds and laughter as they deliver gifts around the world. But don't worry; these farts are filled with festive magic, and they're sure to make everyone smile.

This coloring book is the perfect way to add a touch of humor to your holiday festivities. It's ideal for kids of all ages (including grown-up kids) who want to experience the joy of Christmas in a whole new way. So, grab your crayons, markers, and colored pencils, and let's make Santa's farts the most colorful and festive ever!

Join in the merriment, share a laugh, and bring this wacky world to life with your favorite colors. Get ready for a coloring adventure that's as unique and memorable as Farting Santa himself.

So, get ready to color, laugh, and celebrate the holidays with "Farting Santa's Festive Coloring Frenzy." It's a Christmas tradition you won't forget, filled with toots, laughter, and endless festive fun!

ho ho ho

Fart when someone
hugs you.
It makes them feel
strong.

MERRY CHRISTMAS

hohoho

Let it go; let it rip. Life is too short to worry about silent farts.

MERRY CHRISTMAS

hohoho

Farting is like the song of the body. You might not understand all the notes, but it's a symphony of life

MERRY CHRISTMAS

ho ho ho

I don't always fart,
but when I do,
it's in the most
awkward silence.

MERRY CHRISTMAS

ho ho ho

The silent but
deadly is not a ninja;
it's a fart.

MERRY CHRISTMAS

hohoho

Farting is the body's
way of giving you
an ovation
for your digestive skills.

MERRY CHRISTMAS

hohoho

Farting:
The only moment in life
when you can truly say,
'I blew it.

MERRY CHRISTMAS

hohoho

I used to be a
people person,
but then people farted,
and now I'm more of a
'pets and books' person.

MERRY CHRISTMAS

ho ho ho

A fart is just a
ghost of the food
you once loved

MERRY CHRISTMAS

hohoho

If a tree farts
in the forest
and no one's around
to smell it,
does it still stink?

MERRY CHRISTMAS

hohoho

Don't ever trust a fart
during a job interview;
it might just be
a silent 'Hire me!'

MERRY CHRISTMAS

hohoho

Why did the fart sit down?
It wanted to give
the rear-end a break.

MERRY CHRISTMAS

hohoho

Farting in an
elevator is wrong
on so many levels.

MERRY CHRISTMAS

hohoho

"I don't always
fart in public,
but when I do,
I give it
my best performance.

MERRY CHRISTMAS

hohoho

A good fart
is like fine wine;
it should be savored,
not rushed

MERRY CHRISTMAS

hohoho

The human body
is like a car;
farts are just
the exhaust pipe's
way of letting off steam.

MERRY
CHRISTMAS

hohoho

When you're feeling down,
just remember:
a fart can turn
any situation into
a comedy show.

MERRY CHRISTMAS

Welcome to the world of boundless imagination, creativity, and exploration.

I'm 15minread, an enterprising author from the United Kingdom, and my literary journey is a kaleidoscope of diverse content designed to enrich and captivate readers of all ages.

Children's Coloring Books: Let me take you on a journey through the magical realm of colors and creativity. With a special focus on children's educational notebooks and coloring books, I aim to nurture young minds, ignite their artistic spirit, and make learning an adventure.

Adult Stress Relief Coloring Books: In the hustle and bustle of adult life, finding moments of serenity is essential. Enter the world of intricate designs and soothing patterns in our stress relief coloring books. Discover the therapeutic power of coloring as a form of relaxation and self-expression.

Sudoku Puzzles and Maze Books: Challenge your mind and embark on mental adventures with our Sudoku puzzles and maze books. These brain-teasers are designed to entertain, educate, and enhance problem-solving skills.

Journals for Every Aspect of Life: My journals cover a spectrum of life's facets. Whether you seek daily reflection, mindfulness practices, meditation guides, food diaries, or a repository for cherished recipes, I've got you covered. Additionally, safeguard your digital life with our password logbook, keeping your online world secure and organized.

Puzzle Books: Dive into an array of puzzle books that cater to various interests and skill levels. Whether you're a crossword enthusiast or a connoisseur of brain-teasing challenges, there's a puzzle book to suit your preferences.

As an entrepreneur, I'm dedicated to creating content that not only entertains but also educates and empowers. Each book is a labor of love, crafted to provide an enriching and enjoyable reading experience.

Join me in exploring the endless possibilities of creativity and self-improvement through our diverse range of notebooks, coloring books, journals, and puzzle books. Your feedback is essential in shaping the content you desire, and I'm committed to delivering on your expectations.

Thank you for being a part of our literary journey, and please don't hesitate to reach out with any questions or comments. Your presence as a reader is a gift, and I cherish it deeply.

Warm regards,
15minread